Be a Duck

8 Life Lessons from Our Feathered Friends

By: Wendy Jarvis

Be a Duck
Copyright © 2020 Wendy Jarvis

ISBN: 9781676788966

<u>*Acknowledgements*</u>

I would like to acknowledge the life lessons instilled in me by my family, past and present. I would also like to acknowledge the influences of family, friends, and co-workers. Living, loving, and laughing together has made me a better **duck!**

For many years, I have used the expression,

'Be a Duck'

This expression is a philosophy I have developed over a number of years both in my professional and personal life. Ducks have many qualities that I think people could strive for to better their lives and deal with the people around them. Yes, I said 'ducks'.

I would like to state upfront, that I am not a duck expert nor do I have a degree in animal behavior. I am, however, a keen observer.
I have watched ducks for decades in the wild such as in the creek behind my home, the lake that my parents live on, and in a pond where a good friend of mine lives. Watching ducks makes me happy (most of the time), and I think some of their

characteristics and behavior is both interesting and enlightening.

 Of course, not all ducks are the same and not all duck behavior is applicable to humans. For the purposes of this exploration, I am choosing to focus on the more positive traits of ducks that I have observed, and how those traits or characteristics could be applied to humans.

What I Have Learned about Ducks:

Ducks Let It Slide

Ducks Let It Slide

Ducks do not take rain personally. They do not question where the water that lands on their back came from, nor are they looking for a motive behind it. They just let the rain slide off their back and continue with whatever activity they were doing. I recognize that this is because their feathers are coated in a waxy substance and not a personal decision, but it still has a meaningful lesson for humans.

People use expressions like 'let it roll off your back', 'let it slide', 'let it go', when something is bothering them. If humans could let things roll off their back, like water on a duck's, life would be much less complicated, and people would be much happier.

What if we could let stress, judgement by others, and negativity roll off right off our backs? What if we could stop those things from seeping in 'our feathers' and holding us back?

There are times in our lives when people spit at us. Of course, I do not mean literally, but rather figuratively. When people say something that is offensive or less than pleasant or kind. Like in the work place when a co-worker barks at you for no apparent reason. We need to let those comments slide off our backs just like the rain on a duck's back and not let it 'ruffle our feathers'.

Just like the rain, chances are the negative things coming your way are not personal. When someone is nasty to another or uses a tone that is unkind, it is more of a reflection upon what they are going through than a personal attack on the other. Unfortunately, you may just happen to be at the wrong place at the wrong time, and *'without an umbrella'*.

If you were to have more knowledge as to why someone acted as they did, you would have more understanding, and in some cases, more empathy and forgiveness. If that coworker used a tone you did not appreciate after they had received some bad news or were having a personal struggle, you would be more likely to let the comment go, *'let it slide'*.

Since we cannot possibly know what everyone we have contact with is going through, we need to be able to let things go from time to time. We need to, not automatically assume that we are unjustly responsible for the actions of others. We need to not question ourselves or play the 'victim'.

As a teacher, I tried each day not to take the actions of my students or their parents personally. I would even tell myself that their behavior could be a compliment of sorts. They would act out their frustrations towards me because I am a safe adult in their lives. They can share their 'worst' with me and I will still be there the next morning welcoming them into my classroom. They trust me enough not to hold any emotions or actions that seem beyond their control against them.

I once had a small class of students who had been identified with various learning challenges and behaviors. One day a troubled young man was so frustrated with a task, and life in general, that he threw a chair and almost hit me and used profanity to express himself. I was able to let his behavior and words 'slide' in that moment and remained calm because I knew the situation was not really about me.

Later when he calmed down, he apologized and thanked me for being supportive when he was not feeling in control. I made a choice to respond to the situation and not react.

If I had reacted by yelling and took the situation personally, our relationship, and in turn my ability to help him grow, may not have been able to remain positive.

When something negative or unexpected happens in our lives, we have a choice. We can choose to react or to respond.

Responding versus reacting are two very different ways to handle situations or events we did not anticipate. When we react, it is taking action without thinking, usually with a lot of emotion. Responding, on the other hand, is taking time to think, and then calmly, without emotion, take action that is meaningful. Responding is how conflicts can be resolved. Reacting usually invites other reactions.

If I received news that my job was changing and my boss informed me that I would have to work extra hours, I can choose to react or respond. I can react by yelling, becoming angry and perhaps saying things I might regret. On the other hand, I can take a moment to think of the things I will have to change in order to make the new requirements work. Then I could calmly ask to discuss the situation further and try to come to a workable resolution.

I am certainly not suggesting we take abuse from people on a regular basis. After all, if anything spits on a duck long enough it is capable of turning around and quacking back. We need to stand up for ourselves as needed, but also let some things go when appropriate.

Part of letting go is perspective taking, and part of it is forgiveness. Can you forgive someone who has been rude or inconsiderate to you because 'their stuff' was leaking out? I hope so.

Often, 'letting go', can be easier said, than done. Nevertheless, holding onto the negative energy of someone else will only make you ill or waste opportunities that are in front of you because you are in your head analyzing and planning a response. Letting something go is what you do *for yourself* not the other person.

In a way, by holding onto negativity, you are allowing that person to continue to hurt you and control you. Take that control away by choosing not to react.

Sometimes we can let comments or actions of others to get 'under our feathers'. We might hold onto this negativity and let it weight us down. If, for example, a person you care about and respect makes a negative comment about your appearance, you might hold onto that comment and let it become part of you. You might perseverate about it long enough that you start to believe it. You then in turn, might miss opportunities to meet new people or go places because you are now self-conscious about your looks.

Wouldn't it be great if we could coat ourselves with an oily substance so we could let negativity and stress slide right off our backs?

Unlike ducks, we make a conscious choice about what we 'let slide' and what we let 'get us wet'. There may be some things we cannot 'let slide'. There could be comments that are too offensive or unacceptable to let go. Comments that must be addressed, because not to do so would be to condone the content on subject.

These kinds of comments might be the ones that are offensive to society in general or the social group. The kind of comments that 'cross the line' regardless of the circumstances or state an individual is in. An example of this kind of comment might be the use of a racial slur or ethnic generalization.

The more we can 'let it slide' the less 'wet' we will be by the negative 'rain' of others.

Ducks are Adaptable

Ducks are Adaptable

D ucks adapt to their environment and the different challenges that those environments might bring. Like 'waterfowl' in general, they swim in different bodies of water ranging from ponds and streams, to lakes and even oceans.

Duck are so adaptable that they inhabit every continent on earth except Antarctica.

Ducks swim in the streams where the water is moving rapidly or in a pond where the water is still. There might be waves pushing them or currents pulling them. These different habitats also have different availability of food and different kinds of predators.

All these habitats have different advantages and challenges. So based on where a duck lives or spends time, in order to survive, the duck must adapt. The option to give up or hide in the bulrushes all day is not possible.

Ducks do not bury their heads in their feathers unless they are sleeping. They keep going. Ducks have to brave the weather; cold or hot, wet or dry. The duck's habitat can shape its character and physical characteristics. The Common Golden Eye species defy even the extreme temperatures of the cold Arctic Ocean waters and do not fly south in the winter.

They are able to maintain their body temperature through adaptation. They have special cells in their legs that cool the blood traveling to their feet and then reheat it when it recirculates back into the body. In this way, heat loss is minimized. Many other species of waterfowl relocate or migrate when the conditions become too extreme.

Humans also need to adapt in order to survive, and ideally, thrive. Part of one's ability to adapt is to *recognize* that something needs to change and then have the *willingness* to accept responsibility for our own role in that transformation.

I think humans are better at recognizing that something needs to change, but have a longer way to go in taking responsibility for that change. Most people can identify what is not working in their lives but are often at a
loss of what needs to happen next. Even if they know what needs to change, the task may seem too large or they may lack the confidence that they can manage their role in that transformation.

Change is never easy and is usually a process with many steps. Sometimes that process may even need assistance to get started. In order to get that assistance though, we need to be able to ask for help. That, in itself, can also be challenging.

We probably all have someone in our lives or at least in our community that seems to be in a constant state of despair. They never have enough money or feel stuck in an unhealthy relationship. They may recognize that their spending habits do not match their income or that their partner is negatively affecting their self-esteem, but they do not attempt to alter the cycle. To do so they would have to accept some responsibility for their predicament and be willing to make a change. Or at least, ask for help.

As humans, we need to be able to adapt to not only our environments but also to life events. No one plans to have something Life changing happen to him or her, but from time to time, it does. These are the times where adaptation is even more challenging.

When someone has had an accident that leaves him or her in a different physical or mental state, he or she will need to adapt.

This could mean life continues in a wheelchair or perhaps without sight. Their physical environment may need to change along with their life style and activities. If they were once involved in a particular sport they may not be able to continue with it. At least not in the way they once did.

Something or someone in a person's life might also change and they will need to be able to adapt. It might be that a significant person in our life moves away or even passes away. If there was a lot of dependence on that individual for physical or emotional support, adapting may be more challenging.

Some events might be less obvious but still require adaptation. It has been said that, 'humans are creatures of habit'. We do not like change. Adaptation is a form of change that requires effort and commitment.

Ideally, people want to more than just survive like ducks in the wild, we want to thrive. By definition, thrive is to 'develop well', to 'prosper or flourish'. Having enough to eat and a safe place to live usually is not enough for humans. We want to feel happy and fulfilled in some way.

Adapting for us might mean making meaningful changes to be true to ourselves. Adapting to new surroundings or people in order for us to move further down our life
path. For example, working at a job to put food on the table may not be enough for some people. They may choose to adapt to a new environment at a new job that makes them happier. Perhaps, one partner in a relationship may need to 'adapt' to a different living style when they choose to live with

the other. They adapt not out of necessity to survive, but rather because they want the relationship to 'thrive'.

We have a choice to either, adapt to survive, or thrive.

Ducks Have Balance

Ducks Have Balance

D ucks can swim upstream or down. Sometimes they ride the current and conserve their energy and other times they use all they have to get to where they need to go. If they cannot swim away fast enough from danger they will fly.

Ducks seem to have mastered the idea of balance of energy. They choose what to put their energy into and when. If they need to swim against the current, they do.

They have strength against adversity when needed. 'When needed' is the key phrase. Ducks do not swim against the current just because they can. They are not out to impress their peers or compare themselves to other ducks. Unless of course it is mating season and then that is a whole other conversation.

There are people who have yet to find this balance in their lives. They 'ride the current downstream' giving control over the direction of their lives to either something or someone else, or they choose to go against the current just because they can, because they have something to prove.

The problem with just going where the current or life takes you is that you will sacrifice your sense of self. Being able to choose and make decisions for ourselves is what makes us unique. Few people enjoy being told what to do and when.

Nevertheless, for some people the act of making decisions can be difficult. For others, by not making decisions, they are also not taking risks and they can avoid taking responsibility when things go badly. These 'victims of circumstance' often stay in a cycle where problems repeat themselves.

The problem with trying to prove yourself all the time is that energy isn't used just when it's needed, but all of the time. This strategy also takes from a person's individuality and ability to make their own choices. They end up reacting to others and using their energy on things they really wish they were not.

If we can find that balance between riding the current and swimming against it, then we can choose how to spend our energy.

If you have ever seen a duck, riding the current and floating downstream, you would also notice that their eyes are wide open. They do not ride that current blindly without constantly monitoring when it is time to turn, swim over to the edge for a break, or turn and swim upstream. Ducks are always aware of their surroundings.

Are we always aware of what is going on around us? Enough to evaluate and interact when we need to? Unfortunately, our personal electronic devices have stolen our attention and impeded our awareness of what is going on around us. We are missing opportunities to observe, make connections and have shared experiences. We have put screens in front of our children before they can talk. They watch movies on family excursions instead of looking out the window at the world around them.

On a recent trip to the Shopping Mall I was amazed at the number of people who were able to walk and talk while looking at their cell phone screens 95% of the time. As I briefly sat on a seat in the middle of the mall with a coffee, I was even more amazed as I watched several strollers travel past. If a child was old enough to hold onto something, they had a screen in their chubby little hands. I was even more shocked when I saw strollers that were available to rent with screens built right in the front. So regardless of the child's age, or their family's economic status, they had access to a device. Instead of encouraging children to watch, learn, and interact with world around them, an artificial one was forced upon them. Children learn from observing and copying the interactions that take place

around them. How are they to learn about social language if they are not exposed and part of it?

As relaxed as ducks can look above the water when they are riding the current, their feet are in motion under the surface. Their feet act as a rudder steering them in the right direction.

There will be times when we all want to ride a current now and then, meaning we want to coast and see where life takes us. We need to however, be monitoring what is going on around and inside of us. We will

then know when to take a break or when to turn around or head in a different direction. We also do not want to miss the opportunities that might present themselves along the way.

Unfortunately, too many people live a life of 'reaction'. They let life happen to them, oppose to taking control of it. Then they wake up wondering why they are where they are in life and can feel sorry for themselves.

The opposite can also be true when people spend too much energy trying to control all of life events. They find it difficult to accept when things are beyond their control.

As a parent, having control and being able to manage every situation can appear to observers as a positive attribute to possess. However, spending all of our energy making things 'just right' or 'our way' can be exhausting. In addition, in the process we can wake up one day and wish we had

44

of just enjoyed spontaneous moments with our children.

Ducks also know when they are hungry or tired and they respond to what their bodies need. There are no coffee shops in the pond or personal devices to distract us from our need for rest. Ducks do not stay up late or need to sleep in. There are also no fast food restaurants to tempt the ducks into thinking they need a snack 24/7. Generally speaking, there are not overweight ducks. They find food, as they need it and stop eating when they are full.

What if we slept when we were tired, and ate when we were hungry and stopped when we were full? Eventually we would wake up when we need to, manage our health, and overall, we would be healthier, and happier.

Unfortunately, from an early age we are not taught, or even encouraged, to listen to our bodies. We do not grow up trusting our bodies' signals when it comes to sleep or nutrition. How many children are told, by their parents, that they must clean their plates even though they are full? How many adults sacrifice sleep to watch television or surf the internet? We ignore our body when it tells us we are tired or need to stop abusing it with unhealthy habits like overeating, smoking, or using alcohol.

What about when we are sick? Do we listen to our bodies and rest? When people are starting to feel ill, they often continue to push themselves and carry on with their regular routine and activities. This rarely leads to a speedy recovery and can lead to other people becoming ill. Sacrificing your health in the present can also mean sacrificing it in the future. Poor sleep habits and lack of a healthy balanced diet can lead to serious life threatening conditions.

We also teach our children to continue with their activities when they are feeling ill. We tell them they will be fine and send them off to school or daycare because we need to get to work. By doing so, we are raising a generation that will neglect their health because they do not value it.

As adults, we need to look after ourselves because we believe we are worth it and set an example for the next generation. We need to get more sleep, have less screen time, and put good food into our bodies so that we can live our best lives!

Imagine how different our lives and society would be if people listened to their bodies and honored what they said?

We could live a balanced life in a balanced world.

Ducks Can Right Themselves

Ducks Can Right Themselves

D ucks may dive to the bottom in search of food or dabble just below the surface and be 'tail up', but they always end up with their heads above the water eventually. They have the physical ability to right themselves. More importantly, they know when things are not as they should be and they take action to correct them.

This is a concept, which we as humans, need to learn. We need to recognize when things are 'not right' and do something about it. We do not always seem to know when we are 'upside down', nor do we know how to right ourselves. Parts of our lives can be a disaster and yet many of us do little to nothing about it.

People can be in debt, but continue to spend money they do not have or even have the ability to obtain. As a population, we are sleep deprived and overweight. Many of us work long hours at high stress jobs with little opportunity to exercise sufficiently without giving up sleep. Nutrition can be a major problem. Not because we lack the money or knowledge of how to eat properly, but because we are always on the go.

None of these reasons are excuses, but realities people face in today's world.

Before a person can make a change there needs to be a true awareness of the problem. You cannot change something unless you are aware that it is 'upside down'. For example, maybe your credit cards are all 'maxed out'. This is a problem; you are spending more money than you have.

Once we are able to take an honest inventory of our lives we need to get to a place of acceptance. You need to accept that you have 'your ass in the air' and it should not be there. This acceptance can be difficult for some people. *'I shouldn't be spending more money than I have and need to change.'*

Accepting that things are a mess can bring many emotions to the surface. We may question, 'How did I get here?', 'Why did I let this happen?', and 'What's wrong with me? These feelings can make it difficult to accept the circumstances that need to change.

Do I have a 'problem' or shopping addiction?

After we are aware, we are upside down, and we accept that we should not be, we have to make a choice.

A duck instinctively turns itself up right and carries on. Some people have lives that are upside down, they are aware of it, they accept it, but do not make the choice to do anything about it. What is holding them back? I believe it is confidence. They lack the confidence that they have the skills to make the necessary changes. The emotional skills or mindset to move forward. To pay off your credit cards you will have to stop spending. This may be a problem because you like spending and it will be uncomfortable to change this habit.

Some people might even argue that they do not have the skills to begin with, let alone enough confidence in them. *I can't stop shopping, I don't know how.'*

I believe we have these skills because we had them when we were children. As a child, when things were broken we tried to fix them using creativity, endless energy and any materials we had at our disposal. For the most part, we apologized when we needed to, picked ourselves up when we fell, asked for help if we needed it, and were less aware of, or focused on the judgement of others.

The final part of adapting or changing is making a commitment to the process. We need to invest in the required actions that need to take place. One of the most difficult actions may in fact be is to ask for help. *'I need to see a financial advisor and live within my means.'*

We need to be willing to commit to the changes and accept the responsibility for our role in them. Only then can we move forward.

Change is challenging every step of the way. We have to recognize the problem, accept it, choose to change it, have the confidence in our own skills, and then make the commitment to follow through.

Be a duck and get your tail out of the air!

Ducks Communicate

Ducks Communicate

Communication is essential for a duck's survival. They have over 30 different calls to communicate. They communicate in order to work together and warn each other of danger. The safety of the flock is the number one priority. Communication is an essential skill for animal survival.

The beauty of animal communication is that it is *not selective*.

Ducks do not choose with whom they share information. They want everyone who can understand, essentially other ducks, what is important. They do not keep things to themselves to be superior; they share knowledge freely and fully.

Do we, as humans, do the same thing? Do we freely share our knowledge with anyone who is willing to listen? At work? At school? At home? Alternatively, do we covet information and keep it from others? Is what we gain by knowing something more important than the damage of someone else's lack of the same knowledge?

Sometimes people feel that if they gained knowledge through hard work or trial, the person next to them needs to go through the same process to receive that information. Students might feel that they do not want to share their research because they feel their fellow student needs to give the same time and energy to have that information.

A co-worker might not want to share knowledge they have on how to solve a problem with their colleagues.

Why? Competition? Partly, I think. If we have knowledge that someone else does not, we feel we have 'an edge' up on him or her, that we are ahead. Sadly, that makes many people feel good, even superior.

What if we shared knowledge freely and communication was open so that everyone was on the same page? What if people experienced success alongside us, or even in front of us? How different would our world be?

If you found out how to make or receive a large amount of money, would you share that information fully, or would you try to find a way to profit from having that information? There are many people out there trying to make a profit on others, sometimes even, on their misfortunes.

What about information that would help people lead lives that are more productive? If you had that information, would you share it freely?

Alternatively, would you try to make money by sharing it only once you have been paid for it?

How many people are making money selling health products to others who are desperate for it? There is always some weight loss secret that will 'change your life', but it comes at a price. People are desperate for that kind of information and others are exploiting that need and sometimes their vulnerability.

What if success was not 'climbing a ladder', where the only path was in a straight line, one behind the other? What if that path to success were more like a rock wall with multiple pathways to the top? One where others could be successful with you and climbing higher did not mean leaving or keeping others behind?

What if on that rock wall of success, you were evaluated on how often you reached down and helped someone else up? Or perhaps on how many people you guided up to the same level you were at? Could you also be awarded points for reaching a hand up to seek assistance when needed?

In today's world people communicate regularly using social media, posting opinions and silly photos. Is that real communication?

Communication used to be having face-to-face conversations. Unfortunately, many people will hide behind screens and would rather 'talk' to the world on social media instead of the people right in front of them. Sadly, opportunities for engaging with each other are lost. How many people converse with others in line at the grocery store or in a waiting room at the doctor's office? It is often difficult to even make eye contact with the people a few feet away because they are staring at their phones.

The way ducks are able to survive and exist in groups is through open, free, face to face communication that enables the whole community to thrive.

Quack like a duck for the whole pond to hear.

Ducks Stick Together

Ducks Stick Together

Ducks are not lone creatures. They instinctively know that they are better when they are with at least one other. Wood ducks lay their eggs in nests high up in the trees. Although the mother duck lays the eggs one day apart, they all hatch within 24 hours of each other. In this way, they face the world together. They understand the benefits of having someone by their side. When it is time to leave the nest, ducklings take a leap of faith from the nest, falling down to the forest floor below, sometimes from as high as 70 feet. When the ducklings land in the leaves below they wait until the last of the ducklings has jumped before heading off as a group to find their mother. They do not try to do it all on their own.

In the wild, a flock of ducks will look for food, rest and travel in groups to ensure their safety. During migration, ducks will stop to rest and refuel after using up their energy and food reserves. Since feeding in mass can make the group vulnerable, members of the flock will take turns as lookouts.

Unfortunately, many people consider relying on someone else a weakness. Whether that someone is a spouse, other family members, co-workers or friends. Somewhere along the line, independence and strength became synonymous.

In the duck world if one duck gets sick, another stays with it until it dies. Not because it can cure it, but to protect it and comfort it. If one duck is limping, you will find another duck slowing down to make sure it is not left behind and separated from the group. A book by Jefferey Mason, <u>The Pig who sang to the Moon</u>, recounts the story of a male duck that stayed with its mate long after mating season.

It was later discovered that the male duck would not leave the female's side because she was in fact blind. He stayed to protect and guide her.

It would be wonderful if every human being knew that he or she would be cared for if they became sick. How much comfort would there be if we all knew we would not be left alone to die?

Migrating ducks work as a team to not only ensure their safety but also to conserve energy. They fly in a V formation that allows them to fly faster and farther. When the lead bird gets tired, another member of the flock will take its place to let the other rest. The leader does not push itself until it is exhausted, trying to hold onto some sort of power.

When we see a member of our 'flock' needing rest, do we give them some of our energy? Or, do some people see this need as an opportunity for themselves to 'get ahead'.

The ducks near the rear of the formation will quack or honk to encourage the ones in front. They have learned that when you work together you can do things more efficiently, and encouraging those around us does not hurt either!

Ducks find a partner, raise a family and protect one another. Mother ducks are devoted parents, and protect and teach their ducklings. She teaches her young what they need to survive, essentially how to be good ducks.

They set good examples, they monitor their ducklings' progress and when they are ready, they let them go.

There are some lessons in duck parenting that humans could learn. Do we set good examples?

Do we teach our children what they need to know to survive in today's world? Do we monitor their progress? Are we prepared to let them go?

Many parents today are afraid to teach their children what they need to know to survive. Some lessons are easy and others are harsh.

One important lesson would be how to fail. Parents will go to great lengths to protect their children and prevent them from being hurt physically or emotionally.

We have 'helicopter' parents who hover and guide their children through experiences only ever allowing them to succeed. These parents make sure their son or daughter always 'wins' and rewards every little accomplishment never allowing their child to feel proud of just their efforts.

We also have 'lawnmower' parents that clear their children's path of all obstacles. These are the parents that run their child's mittens to school, depriving the child of the natural consequence of not dressing for the weather.

When we make mistakes, we learn much more than when we succeed. By not allowing our children to fail and pick themselves back up again, we deprive them of the experience of creative problem solving, free thought and the ability to gain confidence and independence.

In our adult lives, we must all face obstacles and challenges. If the path has always been cleared for us, or we always had help to solve our problems, we never develop the skills or confidence we need to solve them as adults.

Denying children the opportunity to fail is denying them the opportunity to learn.

How closely are we monitoring our children's progress? In order to do so effectively we would need to be in the moment watching and guiding them. We could not be looking at our cell phones or be in the next room. We would need to be present in all meaning of the word. Watching. Listening. Participating. Children want and need their parents' attention above all else. When you ask a child if they would rather have a new toy or time spent with their attentive parent, the answer is usually the time.

As parents, do we set good examples? Do we show our children what good humans are like? Do we lead by example to show what it means to be kind, caring, and empathetic towards others? Do we help people who are less fortunate than we are freely, without judging? Even small gestures such as holding open a door or offering to help neighbors, do not go unnoticed.

Children are keen observers who learn by watching and listening to what is around them. Whether we as adults are at home or out in public, the children around us are learning how to conduct themselves and how to treat other people. They learn who to respect and how to interact with people from all 'walks of life'. Do you smile at the homeless man sitting on the sidewalk and say good morning or do you avoid eye contact and ignore their existence?

When an older relative tells the same story for the ninth time do you still listen attentively?

Do we teach our children by example how to take care of ourselves? How to eat the proper things, how to get enough exercise, and how to avoid temptations? Are we creating a healthy path for our children to follow where we are the leader?

We need to lead by example, 'be a mother duck'. We need to teach our children how to have balance in their lives, and teach them how to listen to their bodies.

When our children are ready, do we let them go? Do we let them make their own way in the world or do we 'set them up' to be more than okay?

Children are staying with their parents longer and longer. The comforts of home are taking priority over the feeling of independence. Is the need to stay at home that of the child or the parent?

Are we encouraging our children to 'leave the nest' and make it on their own? To survive in less than ideal living conditions buying groceries on a budget. Many parents today are still doing laundry and making meals for their children that are well into their adulthood.

Parents do not realize the struggles that their children go through, are the opportunities to learn and grow. By 'protecting' our children from the realities of the real world we are 'enabling' them to continue as children and not letting them transition into adulthood.

Birds of a feather need to stick together.

Ducks are Content

Ducks are Content

I don't know if I've ever seen an unhappy duck but then again maybe I don't know what a happy duck looks like either. I have fed ducks and they seem to be happy; happy with the little things like bits of stale bread.

I think ducks are content because they are able to focus on the simple things of life. They are not concerned with what other ducks are doing around them or with expectations that may be put upon them. They do what they need to do, as they need to do it.

Being 'content' is defined as being 'pleased with your situation' or being in a 'state of peaceful happiness'.

What if we took away all the pressure and expectation that is part of our daily lives? If we took away the social pressures, the media judgment, and our 'inner critic'? How much would we gain in terms of contentment?

As humans, we spend a lot of our energy on comparing ourselves to others and striving for some things that are not obtainable. We seek material things to display wealth or status. It is important to many people to feel that they are on par with their peers; or even better. They want to be more successful, wealthier, or more physically fit.

When we buy something new or go to new exciting places, what do many of us immediately want to do? We want to share those actions with our family, friends, and on social media. Is that because we think others will be better off for having that knowledge, or because we will feel better about ourselves?

Are we conscious of the motive behind the photos we take and share? If I am on vacation in a beautiful location and I take 10 selfies, what is my motive? Is it to later recall the experience or prove that I was there to others? I have done some travelling in my time and it is interesting to observe what people take photos of and how many. For some people it is about trying to capture beauty and take a piece of it with them. For others it is about finding the perfect selfie to prove that they had the means to be there. Unfortunately, not many people are just taking the time to absorb the environment and take home a memory that is inside of them.

On a recent trip to Europe I had the opportunity to visit a medieval castle. In one of the large dining halls, massive tapestries covered the walls. Fortunately, there were benches in the center of the room for me to rest my feet. After snapping a couple of photos, I sat down and just gazed around the room imagining being in the presence of royalty hundreds of years ago. I stared at the beautiful pieces of art and imagined the hours of labor that would have went into creating them. I wondered what conversations that might have been shared over the many hours of work. I probably did not take as many photos as most of the other tourists, but I took home with me a memory that did not need to be shared with the world on social media.

People often want to share their success in order to present their 'best selves' to the world. It is a game of comparing my life with yours. My success becomes dependent on the opinions of others above my own. If I am truly content with my life I should not care what other people are doing or try to compete with them. Yet too often we can be left feeling disappointed or envious when we see our 'friends' on social media doing things we are not. We can feel that we should also be going places and buying material objects when we do not really want to or need to.

I am not suggesting that we become stagnant or complacent, and not strive for improving ourselves, but rather, think about the motives behind our actions. Does having an expensive item make us happy? Even if we never shared its existence with anyone else? Do we perform acts of kindness, even if no one knows we did it?

Ducks also do not rethink or over analyze the past or worry about the future. They live in the present. As humans, we can often be stuck in the past or the future in our minds. We can spend too much time and energy contemplating what was or what will be.

We need to give ourselves permission to enjoy the present. To live in the moment physically, mentally and emotionally. Make a memory with our whole

selves for ourselves. My children have reminded me of this gift on more than one occasion. When they have wanted 'just one more minute' to splash in the water at the
beach or when going for a walk took forever because they needed to examine every rock. They are living in the moment. And they are inviting me to live it with them.

When we are enjoying a meal, listening to a story or just spending time with our families, are we mentally and emotionally available?

Or, are we thinking and processing about the past or planning the future? Are we able to let go of any of the emotions that do not belong to the current situation? I truly hope so.

Being content sometimes means allowing ourselves 'to be pleased with our situation' and 'in a state of happiness'.

*'Be a **content** Duck'*

Ducks Know their Limitations

Ducks Know Their Limitations

D ucks fly or swim away from danger. Even perceived danger. They are alert and prepared to escape if needed. Members of a flock of ducks take on the role of guard or lookout ducks. They alert the group by quacking loudly if anything in the bushes or sky moves unexpectedly.

The expression, 'sitting ducks' refers to the two to three week period when ducks cannot fly because they have moulted all of their flight feathers at once to replace the old and damaged ones. To reduce the risk of falling prey to predators during this time, ducks have learned to manage the risk by working together. The Green winged Teals feed in pairs with one duck, with its head under the water feeding, and the other with its head up watching for danger. They work together in an up/down pattern. Redheads will swim together in tight groups taking turns being in the center feeding and being on the outside watching for danger.

Danger does not attract, nor thrill a duck. They work hard to minimize risk and prepare for it.

Do we stay clear of danger? What about perceived danger? Somehow, danger makes humans curious. When we hear a noise, we want to go and investigate. Is that always the wise thing to do? A duck does not investigate a dog barking, it flies away. Ducks trust their instincts and flee to safety. Maybe we could learn from that.

Could we learn to *'lean' away* from danger, not into it?

Somewhere along our evolutionary path, danger has become exciting. People want to feel the danger or at least be witness to it. Do you know people who test the limits of safety? People who like to watch tragic events whether that be in the media or in real life?   People who seek the thrill of an adrenalin rush and take unnecessary risks?

Ducks do not perform tricks as they fly, pushing their limits of flight. They would never fly into a tornado or swim in 10-foot waves just to see if they could. Knowing your limits and not testing them, means you acknowledge the risk involved and value your safety more than the thrill or bragging rights you might earn.

Is there a need for recognition and envy in humans that make us want to push our limits?

I think so. Humans want attention and will do dangerous things to get it if they need to. The rest of us are happy to oblige, watching videos of dangerous stunts.

Maybe ducks do not need to do those things because they know their limitations, accept them and put their safety first. They are content with their lives.

Final Thoughts

Ncone of these observations, ideas or questions are unique or earth shattering. They are, however, intriguing and could help us rethink some basic human behaviors.

Humans have evolved over time and we may have stretched ourselves further from our ancestry roots. I question, however, if all of that growth has been positive. Have we come so far that we have actually regressed in the most fundamental ways?

Are we adaptable and balanced?

Can we right ourselves if we are off balance?

Do we communicate freely and let things slide?

Do we stick together and know our limitations?

How content are we?

We differ from animals because we are capable of higher-level thinking. At what cost? Has the pendulum swung too far? Do we need to go back and make sure we are still doing the basics? Maybe revisiting animal behavior could be a starting point to reexamining some of our fundamental behavior.

Maybe we could all learn to,

Be a Duck!

Made in the USA
Monee, IL
22 September 2020